CRAFTS
for
Accessorising
that look

written by
Susannah Blake

WAYLAND

First published in 2012 by Wayland
Copyright © Wayland 2012

Wayland
338 Euston Road
London NW1 3BH

Wayland Australia
Hachette Children's Books
Level 17/207
Kent Street
Sydney, NSW 2000

Editors: Julia Adams; Katie Woolley
Craft stylist: Annalees Lim
Designer: Rocket Design (East Anglia) Ltd
Photographer: Simon Pask, N1 Studios

British Library Cataloguing in Publication Data
Blake, Susannah.
  Crafts for accessorising that look. -- (Eco chic)
  1. Dress accessories--Juvenile literature. 2. Handicraft--
  Juvenile literature.
  I. Title II. Series
  646.4'8-dc23

ISBN 978 0 7502 6834 9

Printed in China

Wayland is a division of Hachette Children's Books,
an Hachette UK company.
www.hachette.co.uk

Picture acknowledgements:
All step-by-step and craft photography:
Simon Pask, N1 Studios; images used throughout for
creative graphics: Shutterstock

Fabulous fluffy
bangle
Page 14

Pretty pendant
Page 18

Contents

SAFETY ADVICE

When you make any of the projects in this book, always put safety first. Be extremely careful with sharp scissors, needles and pins and ask an adult if you need any help.

Learn stitches
Page 30

Daisy button brooch
Page 10

Dazzling Jewellery

Sparkling jewellery, made of beautiful gems and precious metals, can look like a stunning work of art. But there is a darker side to the production of jewellery, especially some of the industries that mine for metals, such as gold and platinum, or precious stones, such as rubies, emeralds and diamonds.

Jewellery ethics

Mining for valuable materials used in jewellery all too often comes at a great cost to both the environment and the workers involved in their production. Environmental destruction through the use of dynamite and dangerous chemicals is still widespread. Workers are often expected to work in dangerous conditions, and child labour is commonplace in many cases.

Taking responsibility

There is a growing movement among jewellery designers to only use precious metals and stones obtained through responsible mining and healthy conditions for workers. They insist on being clear about their supply chains, demanding to know where and how their metals and stones have been obtained.

As well as being great addition to your jewellery box, the crafts in this book make super presents!

All these fab crafts are made from stuff that usually gets thrown out!

Pretty, not precious

Beautiful jewellery can be made from all kinds of materials, not just precious metals and stones. And by choosing to avoid materials that can cause damage to the environment you can be gorgeous and fashionable, but have a clear conscience too. Jewellery made from recycled materials is even better, transforming you into the Eco Queen of Bling!

Find your inner magpie

So what can you reclaim, reuse and recycle to make the fabulous projects in this book? First of all, you need to find your inner magpie. Look out at home, in charity shops and at car boot sales for anything shiny, sparkly, twinkly and pretty.

Sequins, buttons and beads snipped off old clothes are great. Silky and shiny fabrics from old clothes, ties and furnishing materials are ideal. Fastenings and catches from clothes and broken jewellery are essential. Reworking old, broken or damaged pieces of jewellery is a must. Silk, satin, velvet and sparkly ribbon, braid and cords from packaging are always useful. And scrap paper in pretty colours and textures is endlessly versatile when it comes to designing and making your own dazzling jewellery.

Don't be trashy — recycle!

Charm bracelet

Create this truly personalised charm bracelet using small reclaimed objects such as beads, shells, pieces of broken jewellery, or an odd earring. Each object could have a special significance for you, helping to make this bracelet really special.

You will need

★ charm objects
★ PVA glue (optional)
★ acrylic paint (optional)
★ brush (optional)
★ ribbon or string
★ scissors
★ needle and thread

1

Assemble your charms and make sure they'll be easy to attach to the bracelet. If you like, you can paint some of the charms. To make sure the paint sticks well, mix a little PVA to the paint, then paint on and leave to dry.

2

Measure a length of ribbon or string around your wrist, making sure there's plenty of extra to tie the bracelet on, then snip it to the right length. Cut two more pieces of string or ribbon to the same length.

Recycling ribbons

You can find pretty ribbons in all kinds of places – from gift wrapping and chocolate boxes to packaging for cosmetics. Keep your eyes peeled and always save any scraps you find, so you've got a great selection to choose from!

3

Tie the three pieces of ribbon together in a knot at one end and plait them. Secure the plait with a knot at the other end.

4

Cut a piece of ribbon or string, 6 cm long, for each of the charms. Tie a knot in the end of each of the strings or ribbons and thread a charm onto each of them.

5

Tie each charm to the plaited ribbons and cut off any excess ribbon.

Make sure you ask an adult before you cut up their jewellery!

Why not colour code your charms to match your favourite outfit?

Watch that bling!

Give an old watch a new lease of life by attaching a new, groovy, sparkling strap. To decorate, you can use sequins scavenged from old clothes.

You will need
★ an old watch
★ scissors
★ sequins
★ needle and thread
★ ribbon
★ reclaimed string
★ beads

1 Remove the strap from the watch. If you can't cut the straps off, check the box below for other ways of removing them.

2 Cut two lengths of ribbon that are each between 4 and 6 cm longer than one of the old straps.

3 Sew sequins onto the ribbons to decorate.

How to remove a watch strap

Most watch straps are attached to a little bar at the top and bottom of the watch face. Find the tiny hole in line with each bar. Press a needle or pin into the hole and it should release the bar. You may need to ask an adult to help you. Once the strap is off, slip the bar back into place.

If you really can't get the strap off, pop into your local jeweller and ask them if they can remove it. It should only take a second and they shouldn't need to charge you.

4 Loop one length of decorated ribbon through the bar at the top of the watch and sew on securely. Repeat with the second piece of ribbon at the bottom bar.

5 Cut the string into three pieces that are each 10 cm long. Tie a knot into one end of each of them. Thread beads onto each length of string.

6 Attatch the beads to the bottom bar of the watch and cut off any excess string.

You can sew sequins onto the ribbon to cover up any stitches.

9

Daisy button brooch

Create a beautiful floral brooch using an old tie, a button and a brooch fastener. Ask your dad or granddad for any old ties and search for the perfect button on old clothes. You may need to buy a brooch fastner, unless you can use one from a brooch you don't wear anymore.

2 Fold the tie up in a concertina shape, allowing about 10 cm for each fold.

1 Cut off the wider half of the tie and set it aside for another project; you only need the narrow end to make your brooch.

3 Pinch the centre of the folded tie firmly between your thumb and forefinger and use your other hand to fan out the tie into a flower shape. Sew around the centre a few times to keep it in place.

4

Sew the button into the centre of the flower.

5

Sew the brooch fastener onto the back of the flower.

Button up!

Buttons are fantastic for upcycling. You can use them to make or decorate anything from jewellery and clothes to accessories and furnishings for the home.

How many ways can you think of to reuse a button?

Why not use your brooch to decorate your favourite hat?

Flutterby fascinator

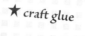

Make a dazzling, fun fascinator by decorating an old hair slide with feathers, sequins and stunning paper butterflies. Funky hair accessories are the latest trend so you'll be truly hip and happening with your hair swept back with this gorgeous hair slide.

You will need

★ hair slide
★ scrap paper
★ pencil
★ scissors
★ craft wire
★ wire cutters
★ craft glue
★ sequins
★ feathers
★ ribbon

2 Cut three pieces of craft wire, each about 7 cm long. Stick the pieces of wire between the smaller butterfly or heart shapes and their larger equivalents.

1 Draw two butterfly shapes and a heart shape onto a piece of scrap paper. On a different coloured piece of scrap paper, draw the same shapes, just smaller. Cut out all the shapes.

Sourcing decorative paper

There are so many different places to find scrap paper that's just perfect for recycling into fab fashion statements. Save scraps of pretty wrapping and tissue paper from gifts and packaging. Tear out pages from magazines where you love the colours and designs. Also always keep decorative paper bags when you've been shopping.

3

Decorate the front top part of the hair slide with sequins.

4

Glue the wired shapes to the back of the hair slide, along with some feathers.

You can stick sequins to the shapes to add more sparkle!

5

In order to keep the feathers and wire in place, stick a length of ribbon across the back of the hair slide using craft glue.

Fabulous fluffy bangle

This beautiful bangle is the perfect way to use up scraps of fabric left over from sewing projects or reclaimed from old clothes. Mining precious metals and stones can be extremely harmful to the environment so choosing to wear jewellery made from fabric means you're really doing your bit to lessen your personal impact on the environment.

You will need

★ decorative fabric
★ scissors
★ embroidery thread
★ measuring tape
★ needle
★ jewellery fastenings

2 Wrap the embroidery thread around your wrist, then add about 9 cm to that length and snip. Tie a knot about 3 cm from one end and thread the other end into the needle.

1 Cut or rip the fabric into long, narrow strips. Don't worry about the strips being identical — this bangle looks better if there is a variety of fabric lengths and widths.

3

Roll each strip of fabric into a loose roll, with the pattern on the outside.

Jewellery fastenings

Always save broken necklaces and bracelets, so that you can reuse the old parts. Hook and eye loops or pull-back catches are ideal for this bracelet, so just look through your collection of broken jewellery until you find one. Snip it off and make it into something new!

4

Thread each of the fabric rolls onto the embroidery thread.

5

Attach the fastenings to the ends of the thread with a double knot.

Why not make individual bangles for your best friends — they will adore them!

Sparkling choker

This super-simple necklace makes the ultimate style statement. Chokers just shout sophistication but are very simple to create. Look out for pretty ribbons on packaging or gift wrap, or maybe you have an old hair ribbon that would be just perfect. Snip the sequins off old clothes and look out for hooks and eyes on the waistband of an old skirt.

You will need

★ velvet ribbon
★ scissors
★ sequins
★ needle and thread
★ hooks and eyes

2 Decorate the ribbon with sequins in any design you like.

1 Measure the ribbon loosely around your neck, then snip to length.

Sew the hooks to one end and the eyes to the other.

Why not customise a party dress with sequins to match your choker?

Dazzling jewels!

Sequins are a great way to add sparkle without impacting on the environment in the way that mining for precious stones such as diamonds can. Think about the kind of look you want to go for. You could sew a simple line of sequins along the centre of the choker, or a line on each edge. You could make a pretty swirling pattern, or just go mad and cover the whole ribbon so it's sparkle, sparkle, sparkle all the way!

Pretty pendant

There's nothing worse than losing a favourite earring... but don't worry! Make this lovely pendant and you can still keep on enjoying your favourite pieces. A dangly earring will work best as you need something big and bold to make a real impact.

1

Decide how low you want your pendant to hang, then cut the ribbon to length, allowing a little extra for tying the necklace on.

2

Thread the earring onto the ribbon.

No ribbon?
Can't find a piece of ribbon long enough? Never fear, you can use scrap fabric instead. Find some old clothes (checking first that you can use them) and cut out three long, narrow strips. Plait the strips together to make the cord for your necklace.

3 Cut three pieces of ribbon, all at different lengths. Tie a knot at one end of each piece of ribbon. Then use a needle to thread beads onto the ribbons.

4 Tie the ribbons to the pendant.

The earring we have used gives our pendant a lovely 'vintage chic' look!

5 As a finishing touch, tie a length of ribbon around the top of the pendant in a pretty bow.

19

Button bracelet

Pretty buttons are great for turning into jewellery. Whether they're made from plastic, glass, mother of pearl, wood or fabric, they're just irresistible. When clothes are past their best, always have a look to see whether you can rescue any buttons. A box of multi-coloured buttons is like a miniature treasure chest!

You will need

- ★ scissors
- ★ ribbon in different colours
- ★ lots of buttons
- ★ needle and thread
- ★ jewellery fastenings

1

Measure ribbon around your wrist and cut to length, allowing for a few centimetres extra at each end to attach the jewellery fastenings.

2

Look through your button collection and arrange your favourite ones in a row to create a pretty visual effect. You might like to layer them, placing small buttons on top of larger ones.

3

Using a needle and thread, sew together any layered buttons.

4

Attach the jewellery fastenings to the ends of the measured ribbon. You could add a pretty bow, too. You can attach it by sewing it to the ribbon.

There are countless different styles of buttons, so this little bracelet can be truly unique!

5

Attach the buttons to the ribbon using needle and thread.

Mobile phone charm

Everyone loves their mobile phone, so why not decorate it with its own personal jewellery? This fun accessory is made from homemade scrap paper beads, but if you have a broken necklace or bracelet, you could reuse the beads from that, too.

You will need

★ colourful scrap paper
★ scissors
★ cocktail sticks or skewers
★ PVA glue
★ string or narrow elastic
★ needle

1 Cut the scrap paper into long, flared strips approximately 20 cm long, 1 cm wide at the top, 2.5 cm at the bottom.

2 Coat a strip of paper in a thin layer of glue, then wrap it around the cocktail stick, starting with the wider end of the strip. Repeat with the other strips of paper.

3

Leave the beads to dry slightly before gently sliding off the cocktail sticks. Leave them in a warm place to dry completely.

The art of rolling paper is called 'quilling'. People make the most amazing flowers using this method!

4

Knot the string or elastic at one end, then, using the needle, thread on the beads to a length of about 10 cm. Tie another knot to keep the beads in place, then tie a loop in the remaining string or elastic.

Upgrade?

Mobile phones are made using rare and precious metals such as tungsten and cobalt. These metals can only be found in very few areas in the world and need to be mined. It's worth reconsidering upgrading your mobile phone regularly to avoid the impact this has on the environment.

5

Attach the charm to your mobile phone or mobile phone cover using the loop.

Friendship anklet

This classic token of friendship is great turned into an anklet rather than the more traditional bracelet. Make it extra special by making it from strips of fabric, ribbon or wool and beads that have special significance – for example from a well-loved old top that's too old and shabby to wear, or a favourite necklace that's now broken.

You will need

★ scrap fabric, ribbon or wool

★ darning needle

★ beads

★ scissors

1

Cut the ribbon, wool or fabric strips into three pieces, each about 30 cm long.

2

Knot together the three lengths of your chosen material at one end and start plaiting them. After every two or three loops, thread a bead onto one of the lengths.

Thread beads onto every length and tie a knot to keep them in place.

Cut one or two lengths of fabric, ribbon or wool for each bead you have threaded onto the plait. Using a darning needle, feed one or two lengths each through a bead.

Once you have made an anklet for your friend, you can teach them how to make one for you!

Throughout history, wooden beads have held a symbolic meaning. In some cultures they are used in prayers; in some civilisations they can be a symbol of rank.

Reclaiming wool

Rather than buying new wool, why not reclaim some from old clothing? If you haven't got any worn-out jumpers or scarves, check out your local charity shop or ask a knitter for their old balls of leftover wool.

Not any old hair band

Transform a boring old hair band into something spectacular by embellishing it with ribbons, sequins and buttons – or whatever else takes your fancy! Who needs a tiara when they could have this stunner tucked into their hair?

You will need

★ hair band
★ ribbon
★ scissors
★ foam sheets in different colours
★ buttons, beads or sequins, to decorate
★ glue

1

Wrap a strip of ribbon or fabric around the hair band, securing it in place using glue.

2

Cut leaf and petal shapes out of the foam sheets.

26

3

Glue the foam sheet shapes together and decorate them with buttons, beads or sequins.

4

Glue the flowers and leaves onto the hair band.

You can use any material that is sturdy and colourful to create these shapes.

Make a style statement!

Accessorising with jewellery is one of the classic ways to really make a style statement. Whether you like it big and sparkly or subtle and subdued, the way you wear your jewellery says an awful lot about you!

Do you want to light up the room like a mirror ball or make an impression with a subdued outfit and single statement piece such as an outrageous fascinator? Do you like everything to have a bit of glitzy glamour, or do you like things cute and pretty? Are you a tomboy at heart who likes a bit of bling in the guise of a mobile charm, or are you the ultimate girly girl who wants sparkle, sparkle, sparkle?

Express yourself

Accessorise your look according to your mood. The joy of jewellery is that you can use it to express the inner you. And when you make it yourself, it has even more of a personal touch. Be flamboyant, be flirtatious, be pretty, be practical. Think about how you feel today, then raid your jewellery box and dare to express yourself.

Try out different looks and try out different pieces on different clothes. A brooch pinned to a plain black coat will look completely different on a floral dress, or fastened to a pretty cardigan. The same necklace and bracelet will look very different teamed with jeans and a jumper compared to how they look with a party dress on a special occasion.

It's all about you! This stunning watch strap looks better than the ones you can buy, and it cost next to nothing. Best of all, its unique!

28

Design your own

The only limits are your imagination.... and the materials you can reclaim, recycle and reuse!

Once you've mastered the basic projects in this book, think about how you could reuse those skills to design your own jewellery pieces. Create an embellished necklace using the same skills used for the charm bracelet on pages 6–7, or create a show-stopping hairpiece with a floral theme using the same basic techniques used for the fascinator on pages 12–13. Make a matching arm cuff to go with the choker on pages 16–17, or make a beaded keyring using the same skills used for the mobile phone charm on pages 22–23.

Craft skills

How to thread a needle

Cut a length of thread. Make sure it is no longer than your arm; too long a piece of thread will become knotted and make sewing hard work. Pass the tip of the thread through the eye of the needle. If the ends are frayed, dampen them slightly. Hold the two ends of thread together and loop into a knot. Doubling up the thread will help to make your sewing stronger.

Starting and finishing a line of stitching

To start, fasten the thread to the fabric using a few backstitches. End a line of tacking with one backstitch or a knot.

Sewing on buttons

Buttons usually have two or four holes, or have a single loop underneath. They need to be sewn on very firmly with plenty of stitches as they are generally subject to lots of wear and tear.

For a two-hole or looped button, sew through the holes or loop onto the fabric about six times in the same direction. Tie off on the underside of the fabric.

For a four-hole button, use the same technique as for the two-hole button, using opposite holes to make a cross pattern.

Tacking stitch

This is used to hold the fabric in position while it is being permanently stitched and is ideal for gathering fabric into ruffles. Pass the needle in and out of the fabric in a line to make long, even stitches.

To make ruffles, do not tie off the line of stitching. Gently pull the thread, sliding the fabric together into gathers or ruffles. When you have created the desired effect, tie off with a backstitch or knot.

Running stitch

Similar to the tacking stitch, the running stitch uses smaller stitches. It is used for seams and for gathering and can also be used to decorative effect, particularly with wool or embroidery thread. You can stitch lines or curling patterns onto the surface of fabric.

Pass the needle in and out of the fabric in small, even stitches.

Whipping stitch

This stitch is used to secure two pieces of fabric together at the edges.

Place two pieces of fabric on top of each other.

Fasten the thread to the inside of one piece of fabric. Pass the needle through both pieces of fabric from underneath, passing through where you have fastened the thread. Stitch through from the underside again to make a diagonal stitch about 1 cm from the first stitch. Repeat.

Blanket stitch

This is a decorative stitch used to bind the edge of fabric. Use a contrasting coloured thread for maximum effect.

Fasten the thread on the underside of the fabric, then pass the needle from the underside. Make a looped stitch over the edge of the fabric but before you pull it tight, pass the needle through the loop. Repeat.

Glossary

Accessory: a fashion item such as jewellery, scarf or bag that can be added to enhance your overall fashion look

Consumer: a person who buys products and services for personal use

Contaminant: a toxic or poisonous substance that infects or soils other substances

Eco: often used in front of words to imply a positive effect on the environment, for example 'eco-friendly' and 'eco-fashion'

Environment: the natural world, including air, soil, water, plants and animals

Ethics: the standards of right and wrong; if something is unethical, it is deemed to be morally wrong or unacceptable

Landfill: also known as a rubbish tip or dump, landfill is a site used for the disposal of waste materials

Mining: to dig coal, metal, precious stones and other resources out of the ground

Recycle: to use something again, usually after processing or remaking in some way

Trend: popular fashion or style at a given time

Toxic: poisonous

Upcycle: to take something that is disposable and transform it into something of greater use and value

Useful websites

freecycle.org: a website helping to keep unwanted consumer goods out of landfill. It brings together people who want to get rid of things and people who need those things.

ebay.co.uk an auction website where you can bid on other people's unwanted goods and possessions.

etsy.com a website where people can buy and sell handmade crafts. A great source for craft inspiration.

Folksy.com a website where people can buy, sell and learn how to make handmade crafts.

recyclethis.co.uk an inspirational website with ideas on how to recycle, reuse and upcycle things that would otherwise go in the bin.

Index

eco chic

Crafts for Accessorising That Look
978 0 7502 6834 9

Charm with your charms
Watch that bling!
Daisy button broach
Flutterby fascinator
Fabulous fluffy bangle
Sparkling velvet choker
Pretty pendant
Button bracelet
Mobile phone charm
Friendship anklet
Not any old hairband

Crafts for Pampering Yourself
978 0 7502 6832 5

Wonderful wash bag/Fruity face mask
Bath-tastic flannel/Rose and coconut bath soak
Luscious lip balm and pot
Perfumed potpourri
Pampering pompom/body scrub
Homemade hair gel and pot
Lovely lavender bags
Funky fish soap dish/Make your own soap
Relaxing bath infusion
Bath bombs and gift box
Vanity kit

Crafts for Revamping Your Room
978 0 7502 6844 8

Beanbag bookends
Dear diary
Personalised door sign
Pretty as a picture
Buttoned wool cushion
Bespoke bedroom cabinet
Bunting
Box of treasures
Sparkling CD hanger
Twinkling window mobile
Owl door stop

Crafts for Styling Your Wardrobe
978 0 7502 6833 2

Tie-d together belt
Not just another plastic bag
Mac makeover
Scarf sensation
Gillet glamour
Perfect poncho
Groovy shoes
Transform a T-shirt
Make a skirt flirt!
Slipper chic
Dazzling jeans

WAYLAND